The Magic Theatre

James Harpur has published eight poetry collections and is a member of Aosdána, the Irish academy of arts. He has won many awards for his poetry, including the UK National Poetry Competition. His books include *The Gospel of Gargoyle* (2024), *The Examined Life* (2021), an odyssey through boarding school, winner of the Vincent Buckley Prize; *The White Silhouette* (2018), an *Irish Times* Book of the Year; *Angels and Harvesters* (2012), a PBS Recommendation and shortlisted for the 2013 *Irish Times* Award; and *The Dark Age* (2007), winner of the Michael Hartnett Poetry Prize. His debut novel, *The Pathless Country* (2021), a historical drama set during the time of the 1916 Easter Rising and inspired by the works of J. Krishnamurti, was winner of the J.G. Farrell Prize and shortlisted for the John McGahern Prize.

www.jamesharpur.com

The Magic Theatre

James Harpur

Also by Two Rivers poets

Kate Behrens, *Transitional Spaces* (2022)
David Cooke, *Sicilian Elephants* (2021)
Tim Dooley, *Discoveries* (2022)
Jane Draycott, *Tideway* (re-issued 2022)
Jane Draycott & Lesley Saunders, *Christina the Astonishing* (re-issued 2022)
Claire Dyer, *The Adjustments* (2024)
Claire Dyer, *Yield* (2021)
John Froy, *The Blue Armchair* (2024)
Ian House, *Just a Moment* (2020)
Philippe Jaccottet, *In Winter Light* translated by Tim Dooley (2022)
Rosie Jackson, *Love Leans over the Table* (2023)
Martha Kapos, *Music, Awake Her* (2024)
Gill Learner, *Change* (2021)
Sue Leigh, *Her Orchards* (2021)
Steven Matthews, *Some Other Where* (2023)
Katherine Meehan, *Dame Julie Andrews' Botched Vocal Cord Surgery and Other Poems* (2023)
Henri Michaux, *Storms under the Skin* translated by Jane Draycott (2017)
Kate Noakes, *Goldhawk Road* (2023)
Alistair Noon, *Paradise Takeaway* (2023)
Ruth O'Callaghan, *Where Shadow Falls* (2023)
James Peake, *The Star in the Branches* (2022)
Vic Pickup (Ed.), *Reading Poets: a new anthology* (2024)
David Ricks, *With Signs Following* (2024)
Peter Robinson & David Inshaw, *Bonjour Mr Inshaw* (2020)
Peter Robinson, *English Nettles* (re-issued 2022)
Peter Robinson, *Retrieved Attachments* (2023)
Lesley Saunders, *This Thing of Blood & Love* (2022)
Robin Thomas, *The Weather on the Moon* (2022)
Susan Utting, *The Colour of Rain* (2024)

By the same author

Poetry
The Gospel of Gargoyle (Eblana Press, 2024)
The Examined Life (Two Rivers Press, 2021)
The Oratory of Light (Wild Goose, 2021)
The White Silhouette (Carcanet, 2018)
Angels and Harvesters (Anvil Press Poetry, 2012)
The Dark Age (Anvil Press Poetry, 2007)
Oracle Bones (Anvil Press Poetry, 2001)
The Monk's Dream (Anvil Press Poetry, 1996)
A Vision of Comets (Anvil Press Poetry, 1993)

Translation
*Fortune's Prisoner: The Poems of Boethius's
    Consolation of Philosophy* (Anvil Press Poetry, 2007)

Novel
The Pathless Country (Cinnamon Press, 2021)

First published in the UK in 2025 by Two Rivers Press
7 Denmark Road, Reading RG1 5PA.
www.tworiverspress.com

General Product Safety Regulations (GPSR) documentation:
www.tworiverspress.com/about/gpsr

© James Harpur 2025

The right of the poet to be identified as the author of this work
has been asserted by him in accordance with the Copyright,
Designs and Patents Act of 1988.

All rights reserved. No part of this publication may be reproduced,
stored in or introduced into a retrieval system, or transmitted,
in any form, or by any means (electronic, mechanical, photocopying,
recording or otherwise) without the prior written permission
of the publisher.

ISBN 978-1-915048-23-3

1 2 3 4 5 6 7 8 9

Two Rivers Press is represented in the UK by Inpress Ltd
and distributed by BookSource, Glasgow.

Cover painting: *The Badminton Game* by David Inshaw

Cover design by Nadja Robinson
Text design by Nadja Robinson and typeset in Janson and Parisine

Printed and bound in Great Britain by Short Run Press, Exeter

Acknowledgements

Poems from this collection or versions of them have been broadcast or published in *Agenda*, *Books for Breakfast* podcast, *The Irish Times*, *Poetry Ireland Review*, *New Humanist*, *Sunday Miscellany* (RTÉ Radio 1), *Studies* and *Temenos*. 'The Active Voice' and 'Final School Report' were previously published in *The Examined Life* (Two Rivers Press, 2021). 'Tryst' was translated into Italian by Francesca Diano and published in *Il vento et la creta* (Molesini Editore Venezia, 2023). 'Revised Myth' was first published in *A Vision of Comets* (Anvil Press, 1993) and won first equal prize in the Powell Prize competition and was a runner-up in the 1979 UK National Poetry Competition.

Many people have given me invaluable encouragement, support and advice during the course of writing this book, and I would like to thank Evie, Grace W, Jules, Lindsay, Lucy, Merrily, Pat, and Rob.

Also my special thanks to Sarah Alyn Stacey, Sarah Binchy, Penelope Buckley, Philip Coleman, Jody Cooksley, Joanna Cooney, Patrick Cotter, Francesca Diano, Sarah Hamilton-Fairley, Peter Longshaw, Mark Roper and Ian Wild.

I would like to thank Cranleigh School for all its great support over the years, and to pay tribute to my teachers, especially Chris Richardson ('Neggers'), Stephen Winkley, John Bain and David Barlow, who helped to get me into Cambridge. I would also like to thank my wonderful and patient tutors at Trinity College, Cambridge, especially Adrian Poole, who helped to set me on the road to poetry. Many thanks, too, to Trinity College Dublin for granting me a Visiting Writer Fellowship at the Oscar Wilde Centre, enabling me to finish the manuscript.

Finally, I'd like to thank Peter Robinson, Anne Nolan and Nadja Robinson at Two Rivers Press for their excellent midwifery.

Contents

Foreword by Penelope Buckley | xi

The Magic Theatre

Prologue

Auditioner | 3
The Active Voice | 6
Final School Report | 7
Letter Opener | 8

Act I: Walking Shadows

Initiate | 10
  1. Entrant
  2. Squatter
  3. Mourner
  4. Anchorite
  5. P.O.W.
Classicist | 16
  1. Remembrance of Tears Past
  2. Brutus
Neighbours | 18
  1. Wittgenstein
  2. Altar Ego
'The Badminton Game' | 20
Heffers University: Zen | 21
Crow | 22
Lecturer | 23
The Oxford Bus | 24
Concert Goer | 25
Christmas, 1976 | 27
Captain Oates | 28

Drama Student | 30
  1. Voices Off
  2. Comedy Routine
Herefordshire | 32
Star Performer | 33
Lost Lover | 35
  1. Breaking Up
  2. 'Afterglow'
  3. Method Acting
Touching the Sky | 38

First Intermission: Ballad of Mont Blanc | 40

Act II: The Burnd Lampe

Brother | 44
Tenant | 45
Tryst | 46
Love in a Cambridge Climate | 47
  1. Fewer
  2. On the Sidgwick Site
Playwright | 49
  1. Chemistry
  2. The Prompter
Scholar | 52
  1. Tutorial
  2. Diviner
  3. On First Finding Jung's *Collected Works* in Trinity Library
  4. Slave
  5. The Weekly Essay
Sic Transit | 57
Ghosts | 58
Orpheus | 59
Refugee | 60
Spectator | 61
  1. Letting Go
  2. Tragi-Comedy

Summer Term | 63
Eleusinian | 64
The Statues | 65
Poet | 67
  1. Revised Myth
  2. Snakes
The Burnd Lampe | 70
Party Animal | 71
Fairy Godmother | 73

Second Intermission: Rough Beast | 75

Act III: Days of Lazy Punting

Questioner | 80
Rocker | 82
Revenant | 83
The University Library | 84
Death of a Thespian | 85
  1. 'The Infernal Machine'
  2. Cast Party
Regretter | 87
Reviser | 88
Sundials | 89
Punter | 92
Son | 93
Slough of Despond | 94
The Eleventh Hour | 97
  1. The Losing Method
  2. The Night before Finals
Endgame | 99
  1. Early Morning before Finals
  2. Final Time
Our Revels | 101
Last Rites | 103
The Magical Universe | 104

Foreword

The Prologue to *The Magic Theatre* recalls a few poems from *The Examined Life* as a starting point for something close to a reversal, for *The Magic Theatre* performs a highly varied and surprising transition from death to birth: a death to the examined life, a birth to something not examinable, the 'I, who may not even be'. The change is exquisitely touched on in lines in 'The Statues', about the funeral vase for a young woman 'led by Hermes / Who takes her gently by the hand / As if to say *death is easy, trust me* / ... her life – / And mine – must start anew, must start anew'. Much of *The Magic Theatre* is elegiac, pained, or informed by dread. It is also full of vitality, puzzling encounters, dialogues both subtle and shouted, indelible characters caught in a flux of moments and affections (Phil, Olly, Marian, Sarah O), exposures to sensation and place. Cambridge is real and unreal, backdrop and stumbling block, felt, seen, almost lived in, certainly passed through. That passage is exhilarating, full of wit and fun, peopled by ghosts.

The first year is the initiation rite: performing blindfold under lights before an audience, in new costumes, subject to the fear of buffetings, and called on for commitments in new liturgies. The speaker performs without a script to other students, in Hall, in someone's room, and then on stage under direction. He stumbles; he sabotages himself; he gains some mastery to become the playwright, author of the scripts. He enjoys hilarious wild parties. He goes to tutorials, one 'a silence of two blokes / ... having a smoke', another a terrifying encounter with an *Übermensch*; he finds a refuge in the Girton College hostel among friends. Yet every fresh experience comes with an undercurrent of evanescence and loss: the family home sold, the long-loved first love painfully withdrawing, the father never more lost than when he's seen. Friends start to dematerialise; Olly, 'his ghost / Still padding through the snowdrifts, / leaving footprints / everywhere

I go'; Jonesy 'lonely / At Oxford'; 'kindly phantoms' at the speaker's coming of age dinner. Behind discovery is a sense of fatedness; behind the playwright is a spectre of a higher playwright.

Yet under all that blundering and wit, something is being born. The unshaped inner being begins to assert itself, to *pass out* through a kind of death. Reading Eliot creates 'A stirring, deep down, or in the dark – / Like our tortoise in the spring, in attic straw'. Jung brings the revelation of (in the manner of Howard Carter finding the tomb of Tutankhamun) *'Wonderful things'*. The speaker writes a poem of his own in which like snakes 'the phrases / Slithered off to find their paths'; as they move, he finds 'An emptying of self, a slipping into the strangeness / Of never knowing what comes next'. By stages, the past can be allowed to be the past, farewelled with a sad ceremony. And although, as Final Judgment Day approaches, the speaker becomes ill with dread, he does pass the Brig o' Dread to experience the unexaminable emptiness of self as 'free'.

The Magic Theatre is at once an entertainment and a mystical progress, sharp-edged, brilliant, and original. The snakes of Harpur's Cambridge slither powerfully and fast.

Penelope Buckley
Melbourne University

For Oliver Slater, Marian Macgowan and Sarah Overton
and in memory of Rob Jones, 1957–2023

> Our souls are love and a continual farewell.
> —W.B. Yeats

The Magic Theatre

He may find in one of our magic theatres the very thing that is needed to free his neglected soul. A thousand such possibilities await him. His fate brings them on, leaving him no choice; for those outside of the bourgeoisie live in the atmosphere of these magic possibilities.
—Hermann Hesse, *Steppenwolf*

Grant I may so
Thy steps track here below,
That in these Masques and shadows I may see
Thy sacred way …
—Henry Vaughan, from 'I Walk'd the Other Day'

PROLOGUE

Auditioner

Pre-Oxbridge interview, Trinity College, Cambridge,
11 June 1974

Too early for this rum ordeal
I wander like a boarder on parole
Dead-ringer for a Fifties pupil –
Ferocious fringe, a Mormon suit,
My shirt unbuttoned at the top
To show the world I do not give a toss –
And yet I'd give the world to act
A student, my waterfall of tresses
Caressing my kaftan as I roll
A fag, a Rizla paper on my lip.
The stage set looks so real! –
The river painted like a moat is slipping
Between its green-suede banks
And tourists syrup along in punts
Jolt-laughing as a pole sticks –
So many tableaux in the town –
On every corner soars a palace
Or tower, spire or ancient wall;
And keyhole cracks in college gates
Reveal a haze of golden courts.

Lord, it is time. Now or never.
The entrance looms like Traitor's Gate.
Set in the castellated tower
The tiny door of Fate
Opens … opens … into Great Court –
So vast! – a harmony of cobbles

Inlaid with emerald parquet lawns,
A covered fountain as its omphalos.
How do I look at such a space –
So unsuspected and glorious?
The winding clopping staircase
Beats out my mugging-up of lore:
If he propels a rugby ball at me
I catch it, slip it back to him
Or kick it in his bin or tray
To win a scholarship or exhibition.
And if he's flat out on the floor
I lie down next to him, start chatting
As if it were quite natural.
And if he says: 'Is this a question?'
I say: 'If it is, this is an answer.'

I knock and enter. Mr Easterling
Is at his desk. Just sitting there.
He lobs me nothing but a greeting,
Gestures to a seat. 'So, James,
What do you like about the *Aeneid*?'
I know my lines – yet it's strange
The way they come out headily –
As if I've breathed pure oxygen –
He wills me on like a horse
Along the final hill at Cheltenham –
I want to say Aeneas's *pietas* –
Descent to Hades, the Styx –
His failure to hug his father's ghost –
But words clunk in Latin syntax,
A hesitation of subjunctives.

Back in the world the river
Slides on and punters iron out
The sheet-light of the water –

The blissful tourists ignorant
Of how my future's finely poised.
Beyond the farther bank a bevy
Of extras playing students glide
Out of the Summer of Love
In sandals and bleached flares –
They look so happy-go-lucky
With their flowing stripy scarves
And beards of scholar-gypsies
They tip me back to Tartarus –
The tantalising vision
Across the stream – so near so far –

Figures moving in sunshine

Sound of playful laughter

Elysium, the Blesséd Ones.

The Active Voice

January, 1975

The school is hushed, asleep.
I'm wide awake, my lamp as bright as Artemis's moon
Above a sea of open books, all Greek.

The voice is nagging me *You need an 'A'*:
Revise another verb. I'm slowing down
But conjugate 'I work', *ergazomai*

And do the aorist of *phroneo*, 'I think'.

Go on, one more my yawn's a silent bellow
For help, the tenses are a labyrinth

Exams are closing in but I will never close
The gap of ignorance, like Zeno's arrow.

One more might make the difference my eyes
Are pink with fear of failure *Don't go to bed*

Alright, just one … *phobein, phoboumai* 'dread'.

Final School Report
15 July 1975

It's like I've stumbled into someone's funeral,
Mourners whispering to each other
Around the flowered coffin in the graveyard.

Barlow: 'Undoubtedly it was hard for him
              to make up all that lost ground …'
Megahey: 'The break in continuity went deeper
              than I thought …'
Neggers: 'I was alarmed to find how far his absence
              had affected his development.'
Corran: 'One hopes that he will gain the grades.
              I fear his illness has set him back too much.'

I close the report, like a lid, to shut their voices out.
But the mourners stay whispering …
Becoming less distinct
As if they're walking away or I
                            am inching down
Into the darkness
                of another life.

Letter Opener

4 August 1975

My mother's left it on the window sill;
The hallway has a dusty summer glow.
She's made herself scarce, is with me still.

The envelope's utility-bill beige.
I pick it up and feel that even now
The Fates are in the midst of change –

As if the future's in the balance
And they are magically rewriting it –
An 'A, two Cs' … a 'B, two As'? –

And only when I slit it will they stop.
I rip the paper, take the letter out,
And see the rush of words caught on the hop

Like ants beneath a stone – until they click
Into a future, irrevocably fixed.

ACT I

Walking Shadows

Whewell's Court
September 1976–June 1977

Remember: you're an actor in a drama of the sort the author chooses ... For this is your business, to act your given part well. But when it comes to choosing this part – that belongs to another.
—Epictetus, *Enchiridion*

The mirror does not flatter; it faithfully shows whatever looks into it – namely, the face we never show the world because we cover it with the persona, the mask of the actor.
—Carl Jung, *Collected Works*, Vol. 9, i.

Initiate

1. Entrant

3 October 1976

Can't believe it's happening again:
Dad's silent car, a trunk of ironed fears –
But now we trade school kitchen bins
And fire escapes and concrete stairs
For the Hampton Court of Trinity.
Car doors slam, roof-racks unstrung,
Hugs and handshakes, and 'Mother'
Replaces 'Mum'; I need a smile, an omen –
Oh for my 2 North Senior Dormitory!
The rush upstairs to dump my trunk
And bag a bed beside dear Jonesy –
The aura of my princely rank
Pouring from my shoulders like a glory
In the eyes of little Fourth Formers.
Now entering this giant Tudor folly
I have a walk-on part, a spear-holder,
Must learn the small talk of the serf.
The unpeeling vision of Great Court
Reduces Dad to gibber-jokiness,
His brain a bat consuming flies at night;
He calms himself, recites his fantasy –
His son an actor on this stage of dreams
And he who used to be a lift boy
Will toast *such* crumpets in his rooms.

These are perhaps the final moments
Our worlds will still connect
Before I get more bookish by the month
And make him feel inadequate –

Yet revelling in the image of his son
The Cambridge boy! at which I'll sneer
Until approaching death he'll let on
From the cosmos of his wheelchair
That he could only pay my fees
By gambling. Roulette in Kensington.
And still I will not credit him
Until the croupiers come to his cremation
And talk about his courage and will:
Then I'll see my fate was balancing
On ventilated breath, a spinning wheel,
A father's love.
                We snatch a hug and kiss
And I'm relieved he's going, yet sorry
He's taking off my last scrap
Of homeliness … familiarity.
I turn to take the plunge, turn back
To see his bald head, puffy face
Grinning like a headlight
Along the road to London and relief
Of reaching his old habitat:
The Garrick Club, his Chelsea life,
The scented leopard skin of his new wife.

2. Squatter

In K5 Whewell's Court

Blackstained as if by bathroom mould
The Gothic annex made of rain
Rises high through clouds across the road
In central Transylvania …
Grope through mizzle – there, my name
In gold! – *you're not an admin error.*
Up stairs, knuckle-knock door
To exorcise the previous freshman's ghost
From what is now *my* desk, *my* chair,
Gas fire to toast marshmallows,
Some flimsy cafeteria furniture,
A window view of Sydney Sussex.
Drop bag down like an anchor
From a ship of 20,000 passengers
That's turning slowly in a circle …

Missing home (is Mum about to sell?),
Nail teenage years to walls
In kilims, posters; keep repeating mantra
I am my name in gold calligraphy
I'm now an undergrad
Go giddily
To bedroom, test out bed –

Shut eyes, flop backwards gently as a kiss

And fall, fall
           into the abyss.

3. Mourner

My mother's letter is as cold
As a bored solicitor's –
Regrets to say the house is sold,
Just thought I ought to know.
Right now I'm far too far away
To grieve, or feel what *she* is going through –
I'll know this only in the future
Unpicking phrases in her diary:

I had originally visualised
Long Acre as my family home
Where grandchildren would visit me.
We stayed for only twenty years.

Only twenty years? My lifetime!
Delivered there by Dr Scurlock
One foggy morning in December.
My DNA's in every speck
In every room, in every corner.

No sadness for me now –
But that will come ... and come once more
When reading of Mum's final day:

The house is empty and has lost its homeliness.
Removal men from Luton come at 10 a.m.

After the van drove off I had a good cry
And walked around the garden picking flowers.

4. Anchorite

Matriculation Dinner, 6 October 1976

Mead hall, cat's cradle of black beams,
Rows of caramel-sheeny tables
Agleam with tiny lights, gilt cutlery.
Bejewelled and porcine Bluff King Hal
Stands mightily across the room,
Gloating from his picture frame
As if to crow he's eaten all our food.
A hush before Black Gown says grace:
Oculi omnium in te sperant Domine …
I sit – then leap up as a voice replies:
Et tu das escam illis in tempore …
So far I've heard more Latin than English.

Alumni in the paintings spur me on
To chip in to the larky repartee –
Sir Isaac Newton, Herbert, Dryden?
Tight-lipped I wonder if they would believe
The slouching beatnik, two along,
His lolling locks as greasy as his food
Who tells us that his name is Byron?
And, opposite, the chirpy witty lad
Who says he's Coleridge? I screw my courage
And quip 'Where's Shakespeare?' – *far too earnest
As if I'm asking 'Where's the Gents?'* –
But someone takes me at my word:
'Oh Nick's at Magdalene, English Lit.'
*Smile, nod as if you knew it all along.
Then take the veil, become an anchorite;
And if you have to speak: act dumb.*

5. P.O.W.

It has the feel of going to a zoo:
'The rare blue-gowned Etonian.'
But I'm as edgy as an interviewee
In this friend of a friend's den
Of paintings, set of Gibbon, candelabra;
He's perching on a low-slung sofa,
High forehead off a cameo brooch.
A sleeve of navy velvet pours Madeira
Not sherry into fluted crystal glasses.
I lean forward, crossbow primed
For condescension; but he's modest.
I want tall tales of Pop, the Wall Game,
But get affairs political –
Riots in Indian cities. 'Turban violence?'
I mutter. He laughs. I've passed my oral.

He lends me his old gown for Formal Hall
And introduces me to scholar-cronies
A yawn or two from being full professors –
They watch me with such scrutiny
It sparks my old recurring nightmare:
A prisoner escaping Germany,
A train, a Nazi offers me a cigarette –
I take one, murmuring a fatal *'Thank you'*.
Here my false I.D.'s still watertight
Then someone asks what school I went to –
Like one of H.M. Bateman's cartoons –
'The boy who went to a minor public school!'
I murmur *'Cran*leigh?' ... silence perfuses
The air like a blush. 'Good school. I know it.'
He smiles as if he's patting my shoulder.
I don't care if he's being diplomatic –
I want to scream, *'Danke, danke, danke!'*

Classicist

1. Remembrance of Tears Past

Fifteen of us with photocopied sheets
Of Sophocles; a lanky lad from Blackpool,
Shy, twitchy, is 'invited to translate' –

The Greek swarms over me like eels.
The silence forms a crack and then a hole
I'm tumbling down, head over heels

Until I hit a memory – aged four,
First-ever day at Heath House School,
A circle of us sitting on the floor

A girl is singing 'Twinkle, twinkle little star' –
I twist it in my head I'll have to sing as well –
I shut my eyes to make the world go dark

Then hear a little voice beside me trying
To be heard: 'Please Miss, the boy's crying.'

2. Brutus

On meeting a delegation of my old school teachers,
25 October, 1976

A chandeliered function room in Caius –
    And there they are! corralled together;
Their fingers pincer sherry glasses
Like sticks of chalk – no longer gloomy masters
    But twinkly pink-faced giggly scholars –
I thought I'd waved goodbye to them last summer
And now I'll have to do it all again –
    But with the added squirm of Christian names:
Dunnett is Ray, McGahey, Alan,
And head of Classics, 'Negs', is *Chris!* –
    I was his raison d'être in a class of one –
The door shut like an Iron Maiden's lid –
Two years of spiky intimacy
    With Homer, Virgil, Sophocles.
His pouting smile's still stuck on his face –
How can I do the deed? I've been rehearsing it
    All week – my Brutus stab –
'I've changed. I've changed to English Lit.'
Carpe diem: I sidle up –
    He beats me to it. 'Dropped your Classics?
Now that's a shame …' *Come on, erupt!*
I dip my eyes as if to blame the sherry
    And feel like a soul who's failed in Hades
Now standing in the sludgy ferry
Re-crossing the Styx, and looking back to spy
    The shades of Homer, Virgil, Sophocles,
Waving him goodbye.

Neighbours

On K Staircase, Whewell's Court

1. Wittgenstein

Begins as just a word
Three syllables
   I tentatively mouth.
   Becomes a rumour:
A Viennese philosopher
Obsessed with language
   (I think) and poised
   Between genius
And nervous breakdown
(Someone tells me).
   Becomes an image –
   Curled up on his bed
Foetally
In the tower
   Three floors above me;
   Or looking from his window
Over rooftops
Towards the spires of King's.
   Becomes an atmosphere
   On Sundays
When Universe is quiet,
A set of footsteps
   Passing my door
   As softly as a cat's
Ascending to the top
Where he reverts
   To image; rumour; word.

2. Altar Ego

A shiny-eyed medic, Born Again,
His cherry lips as glossy as his brogues,
Keeps pestering me to go to Evensong
And is obsessed that I should know
His sexual errancy: I become
His personal chaplain, twitchy confessor,
And take to tip-toeing past his rooms
In case he lurches from his lair
To grab me. He wears me down.
Perhaps he's an agent of destiny?
And what's the worst thing that can happen?

We set off to his church one evening
And squeeze together in a pew.
The minister announces: 'Great tidings!
The spirit is *here*!' My neighbour prods me –
His lips sucked in to an expectant bud.
The minister calls for God's lost lambs
To take the plunge and come up to the altar –
I feel a fleshy finger jabbing at my ribs.

And in my mind I do not falter:

Praising God for giving me the strength
I rise and march along the aisle towards
The exit
        and darkness over Market Square
A blessèd southern wind
                and God's own stars.

'The Badminton Game'

David Inshaw Exhibition, Wren Library, autumn 1976

For David Inshaw and Peter Robinson

I step inside the mind of Wren and find
I'm in his blueprint for this library:
Dutch interior floor, neat window panes,
Coolness and light beyond the physical:
The perfect order of the printed lines
Of printed letters in each leather book.
No echo, breath or trace of anyone.
Inching along a row of paintings
On display I turn the corner of a frame –
And stumble into someone else's mind
Or someone's dream, as if I'm parting leaves
And staring at a childhood paradise:
A Big House garden in high summer –
Two girls in deep magenta dresses
As light as shuttlecocks in evening air –
The only souls within a slow conjunction
Of elements   a moon with seas of dust,
A pale blue sky, shoals of cloudlets
And shadow lines of hedge and house
Soft-shifting in the fall of evening.
I want to stay forever, watching
The girls play badminton forever
Inside a mind, inside another mind.

And then I realise both are now in mine.

Heffers University: Zen

A squall of sleet pours slush
On Vladivostok-on-the Cam
Sloshing the Blue Boar and Caius,
But Heffers is so carpeted and warm,
Soft-lit and blissfully un-Gothic.
From level to level, case to case,
I glide to spines of hippy books –
Like Castaneda, *The White Goddess*,
Siddhartha, *Gormenghast*,
And open up *The Way of Zen* at random
(Except is anything by chance?):
'Our precious self is just a notion,
Useful and legitimate enough if seen
For what it is, but disastrous
If we identify it with our real nature.'
I want to eat that sentence.

My precious-self-idea puts back the book,
Extracts my actual body
To actual pavements and *The Whim*
Wherein whatever self that's me
Dissolves in warmth   a background hum
A helping of moussaka, chips ... and Om.

Crow

Ted Hughes's 'Crow and the Sea'

I try to stalk this strange new bird:
It perches on my desk – an inky blot
I lunge at – it slips away, flies off
Only to greet me in the morning,
A patch of night I just can't grasp.
I try to junk my querulous thinking
And *listen* to it. Why can't I listen to it?
Is 'Crow' a crow, and 'sea' a sea?
I try ignoring it, then talking to it;
I try hating it; I want to hear it *caw*.
But still it's just a silent murmuration
Within the sky of paper. Until I yield
And stand and watch it, struck dumb.

Like a scarecrow screaming in a field.

Lecturer

First English lecture, 25 October 1976

Tall, gowned and lethally saturnine,
Slicked-back hair a wavelet on his collar,
Sideburns of Victorian perfection,
He flashes on an overhead projector:
'Jack and Jill went up the hill ...' A laugh rises
And takes two barrels of his eyes.
It could be Thomas Arnold's Latin class.
'So, Jack and Jill went up the hill. Why?
To fetch water. Note, they simply *went*.
They didn't dawdle, nor were they in a rush.
And *Jack*, not Jill, incurs the accident –
Why him not her? The poet doesn't tell us.
We must infer from the lacunas ...'

Then later on that day I go to Heffers
And spot the lecturer's book of poems:
Peeping inside its pink metallic cover
I read the title poem three long times:
'Pink star of the languid
  settles by a low window
lap to flit, give the life
  too quickly, the storm
a mere level gaze ...'

I note the star is pink, not cerise,
The window's low not high, and that's not this
And that's not that ... but not *what is* –
'Pink star'! 'Jack and Jill'!
Eheu, Virgil – what have I done?
My head throbbing from this poetry caper –
I tumble out of Heffers to wrap my crown
In vinegar and brown paper.

The Oxford Bus

28 October 1976

We're dieselling through the Midlands
The Fens unflattening to contours
Depots come and go with airbrake-hiss
A stretch of legs, return to fetid air,
Landscape darkening the windows;
Absence makes the heart grow panicky –
What if we're cool, self-conscious?
And Oxford! *I'll feel like a Confederate spy.*

She meets me off the bus – it's as it was –
All kisses – puppies – haven't changed at all!
She leads me under street lamps
To silhouetted L.M.H.
And in the door-shut hush of her room
Her mask drops – crumpling face –
Her father's death, me, work, friends and so on –
The present is a sucking marsh
From which no future hope can drag her –
But it's the future I foresee next night:
She's starring at the Playhouse, *Charley's Aunt* –
And though escaping in a random part
She looks so radiant with this alien cast
That next day when our parting kiss goes on
So long I have to run to catch the bus
I jam the thought that it's already gone.

Concert Goer

Brahms' *Requiem*, St John's Choral Society,
11 November 1976

November stars of street lamps light
The pavement from Trinity to John's –
Another massive Tudor rampart-gate –
Just me and Belinda, my companion,
Old-fashioned, cream high-collared dress,
Her hair so golden, shimmering;
A silver clutch bag, silver sandals;
Her arm loosely laced through mine.
Belinda – I met her only yesterday
In someone's rooms, an almost-stranger's friend –
Perhaps she's wondering, like me,
If Fate is working through a *Requiem*.

The black-draped angels in the choir
Lie deep within the curve of the apse.
I've never heard the *Requiem* before –
Dark shavings of cello, double bass,
And layerings of violins soften me …
The choir intones a long deep-lung vibration
Dissolving every shred of I –
And everything evaporates beyond
A world of mere appearances –
A stumbling into the holy –
The *Urgrund* – the fountain of being,
The great tuning of the soul …

The baritone's singing 'We shall all sleep
But in the twinkling of an eye
We shall be changed' – there is no me
To change … until the music stops, and I

Escort her out, and watch her cycle
Across the bridge past Magdalene

Her white dress like a comet trails

A fan of sparkles falling, fading, fading

Christmas, 1976

When I left my childhood home to go to college
   It felt like it was sold behind my back –
To spare me from acute nostalgia.
Now strangers are discovering the summer house
   In winter, the monkey-puzzle tree,
The silver-birches Dad designed as goal posts.

Christmas is upon us – it's the first
   I've ever had without a home … and yet
I'm still so close to home that I can see it:
The snow outside our kitchen after midnight,
   The outline of the rose garden and bird table,
A shadow like a fox's taking flight …
Can hear the crush of boots, a whistled tune –
   And there, a crate of bottles like a miracle,
And each one topped with a silver moon.

Captain Oates

Lent Term, 1977

For Oliver Slater

We raise each arm alternately
And synchronise our snow-caked boots
To pad across Antarctica –
Me (Wilson), Bowers, Scott and Oates –
No longer feeling toes and fingers.
Later on, inside our tent
We listen to howlings of blizzards.
Then Oates declares he's going out
And may be some time.

Each night I'm in the wings with Oates
And something in his smile
And shared ironic twitch of eyebrows
When Adrian shouts, 'Think *frost*!
It's minus 40, not the damned Sahara!' –
Creates a bond. A friend at last.
Olly of Magdalene, second year,
A shy wild bird from Highgate,
His profile, Mr Punch; his bush
Of hair sprouting from his airforce coat
Like a thrust-up chimney brush;
His glasses misting up from tea
Or fags. I loved his scepticism –
The way a blinking of his eyes
Could change my view of someone.
'Good golly it's Olly!' I'd shout out
On meeting up at Trinity
Or Magdalene bar, when drinking late.
'All life is Eros, Thanatos,' he'd sigh.

More Thanatos with him, I feared.
His will and energy unmanned,
His essays only half a page.
His scraped degree freezing his dad.

How does a friendship end?
A letter, phone call, more lacklustre?
I didn't want to lose him –
Invited him to stay in Wiltshire.
But just before he came the snow
Fell and fell – he phoned from Waterloo –
I had to say: 'The roads are no-go.
Impassable. We cannot fetch you.'
A silence. 'Yeah, sure.'
                      And that was it.
He walked away, but left his ghost
Still padding through the snowdrifts,
Still leaving footprints
                          everywhere I go.

Drama Student

1. Voices Off

Audition at the Cambridge Arts Theatre, 10 February 1977

I don't know what's goading me
To be in plays – a daemon's voice
Insisting I must battle being shy?
I can't act – too wooden and self-conscious;
And why be someone else at all?
Yet now my startled rabbit self stares
At the director, back of stalls,
Recruiting for *Bartholomew Fair*.
He shouts, 'Take off your jacket.
Go and sell it to a passerby.
Bit of cockney patter. *Off you go.*'
I take my jacket off, wield it feebly
And not a squawk emerges from my mouth.
Invisible pedestrians ignore me
Until I growl like the Artful Dodger:
"Ere you go my lovely – fancy a jacket?'
"Ere you go my lovely – fancy a jacket?'
I sound like a parrot with Tourette's
Then morph into 'pirate' with a lilt –
"Eeer ye go moy luvverly – fancy a jacket?'
I'm in some hell I can't get out of –
As if a disincarnate accent has possessed
My soul – but then I hear: 'Stop! *Enough!*'
A note of panic in the timbre.
I slink off stage, find the door, and breathe
The genuine trader shouts of Market Square …
Stop. Enough.
The tinnitus of humiliation
Echoes still – those words, that voice
None other than my own.

2. Comedy Routine

The Venetian Twins, ADC Theatre, 24 February 1977

I wait in the wings, a menial extra;
My first words on a Cambridge stage –
'*I due Gemelli*' – will start the drama.
So proud! The ADC! A proper play!
My face all sheeny beige with greasepaint –
And I so bonded with the cast –
A jocund company of Venetians
In velvet breeches, silken caps – and poised
To bask in rows of spotlight-eyes
Especially of a girl from Hammersmith
Who's come to see my speaking debut.
Lights go down – I'm on! – but smash
My head against the scenic arch and stumble –
The world swirls to mush –
'*I due Gemelli*' sounds like 'I'm a jelly' –
My friend flushes out a gurgle of laughs
Pursuing me off stage – each scene
I enter to remove a prop she still guffaws
As if I'm practising a clown routine –
I dread my every entrance –
The sudden faces, burst of laughter,
The footlights shining in my brain –
The tool of an interrogator
To whom I swear I'll never act again.

Herefordshire

Easter holidays, 1977

We're staying in a country of small farms
Enfolded into hills and combes, with buds
Remembering trees they left last year.
And everywhere we walk I hear
The plangent oboe notes of *Hergest Ridge*
As if borne by breezes from the marches
Of Wales. At home on this bohemian farm
With Weazle the cat and Felicity
Casting our futures through the zodiac
We try escaping from our lives:
Your father killed just over a year ago,
The bomb outside your house re-primed
Obsessively ... My father in his afterlife
Of second marriage, and Chelsea flat;
My mother selling my childhood home,
Your mother selling your shattered house.
But none of this explains
Your sudden sobbings in the evening
And trance-like gazing into space –
What is it that your third eye can see
Or sixth sense pick up – like the cat's ears
Prickling at a noise outside the room?
We've loved each other for years. But now
We're poised between an ending and beginning –
And I know you know some future thing
Too terrible to talk about inside;
Or outside – on walks among the swallows
From Africa, discovering their nests
In all the barns of Herefordshire.

Star Performer

Easter Term, 28 April 1977

This new audition's just so scary
Self-consciousness has fled
And left a body void of nerves
In tune with the director's words:
'So first a yokel chewing straw
Wooing his childhood sweetheart.
Then give me some Orlando.'

I plunge into an ecstasy of voices
And gestures … then shrivel back to me.
'Brilliant. You've got Orlando.
And Greta Avrimov's Olivia –
Fantastic actress, semi-pro.
She won't *believe* a freshman is her lead.'
His words sting like spittle. Semi-pro?
Greta Avrimov? She *won't* believe …
I want to shout: 'No, *no*' –
That wasn't me performing then –
I just do walk-on parts.'
Yet if it wasn't me, *who* auditioned?
I beam … and exit, pursued by a fear.

Next morning I can hardly move.
My old sciatic injury's flared –
My back and stomach seem to touch in spasm,
A bony cage of agony.
Days come and go – I barely leave my room.
A corset bolts me like a mannequin,
The physio says I'm like hard dough.
I keep on missing the rehearsals …
Until my part's exchanged with that of Oliver.

Overnight my spine heals.
Who are these warring selves –
The one insisting I should lose
Myself in roles and not be 'me',
The roles the other wants to sabotage?
Two selves, and I, who may not even be?

Lost Lover

1. Breaking Up

She wrote to say she had to see me;
A friend was driving up to Cambridge.
So now we're by the river, nervy,
A picnic on the Backs beside the college,
The clouds so high, the chestnut trees
Believing they'll be green forever.
She says she's not sure why she's doing this.
She loves me – not the issue, no, never.
A friend was driving up to Cambridge –
'We're too apart, we must pursue new friends',
New this, new that – she fiddles …
While years of love are burning to their end –
The letters, parties, heart-to-hearts,
The grieving for her dad.
We talk ourselves to mutual silence
Tumescent with unspoken words.
   I walk her back to Trinity gate:
The 'friend' is standing by his car,
A Triumph open-top. She shouts:
'I told you – King's Parade, not *here*!'
And starts to cry. I hand her over –
A baton in the saddest-ever relay race.
They roar off in the getaway car –
I almost hear the clank of cans
Tied to the bumper – towards new lives.
Students are having desultory chats
Outside the sunny lodge, or chaining bikes.
A porter's pecking at a cigarette
Remembering a private pleasure
Like a jackdaw
Inspecting roadkill at leisure.

2. 'Afterglow'

from Genesis, *Wind and Wuthering*

Why is self-pity
So bitter, yet so sweet?
The pleasure of the Fates against you
The direness of a sudden saddened heart
That sucks in every other indefinable loss.
I should be grieving with John Donne
Or 'In Memoriam' or Keats's odes.
But I play the latest Genesis again –
Inserting the stylus on the final song
With a darts player's precision –
Like the dust that settles all around me
I must find a new home …
I sing along and plunge to all that's gone:
My Weybridge teens, family house,
My cycling off to discos
Embedded in every bump of Chestnut Avenue
And the footpath to the tennis club –
I can see its lake surrounded by the wood
Abutting jungle-gardens of the wealthy –
The cage with two Siberian tigers flaming
Our kisses in the rhododendron bushes
And endless paths among the trees
Where now *I would search everywhere*
Just to hear your call
And walk upon stranger roads than this one
In a world I used to know before …

3. Method Acting

(As Oliver in *As You Like It*, Christ's Fellows' Garden, 9 June 1977)

Wandering in the forest of Arden
I sense I didn't sway the audience
That I was plotting against Orlando

And also failed to sound repentant
Of evil deeds – more like a schoolboy
Pretending to be sorry he's late.

Now, at the ending when the lovers
Pair off and interlace their hands
And dance with glowing happiness –

In the spring time, the only pretty ring time,
When birds do sing hey ding-a-ding ding –
I'm rapt by Hymen, who's pronouncing:

'You and you no cross shall part,
You and you are heart in heart,
You to his love must accord …'

And picturing my love a stranger stole
So lately, I bite my lip and smile.

And no one knows I've played my finest role.

Touching the Sky

St John's May Ball, 14 June 1977

I fidget by the gate for brother John
Who crashes May Balls like Houdini –
I'm in a Fred Astaire white-tie from Oxfam
My arm around a nurse called Mandy –
Mature, comely, hennaed hair pinned-up,
Patchouli fragrance like an aura –
Then John materialises, waving tickets
As if he's plucked them from the ether.

We're through! The braziers on the lawns
Shoot spiky shadows across the grass
To creeper-scaly Gothic walls.
Mandy's an agony aunt who hears my woes
Of heartbreak with her soothing *'Aws'*...
She smoothes tiger balm into my temples
And whisks me off to promenade ... and gaze
At rocket trails of fizzing golden eels
Along the Cam below the Bridge of Sighs
And through a jumble of bumping punts;
The world is lifting
And we are floating to the music tent –
Behold, a vision! Afro-nimbused Mungo Jerry –
'In the summer time, when the weather is hot
You can stretch right up and touch the sky
When the weather's right
You got women, you got women on your mind ...'
We dance and jump and touch the sky
For hours it seems on end – the darkness
Receding imperceptibly
                            to Dawn's gold eye
Burning off the walking shadows ...

I feel my first year drawing to a close
Uncertain what I have to show for it –
I'm brimming with prose and verse
But empty of love; my wine-stripped self
Now shrinks from a double quarantine
Of holidays in a temporary home –
It's like the wreckage of a play
After the curtain falls and house lights sweep
The auditorium, returning the cast
To dressing room … stage door
                                  from which they creep

Sans costumes, props and masks.

FIRST INTERMISSION

Ballad of Mont Blanc

i.m. Marian 'Boobela' Myers (1927–2024)

Hurtling down an autoroute
    Aunt Boobela, Mum and me
Are heading for the Italian coast
    Crammed inside a Mini.

Before we reach the Alpine mass
    Mum's poised to be the driver
To save her sister from fatigue
    And panicky claustrophobia.

But as we close in on Mont Blanc
    We see we cannot stop –
Next thing we're bolting into Hades,
    A billion tons of rock –

As if we're in the Perseids
    The tunnel lights flash past
And lorries looming up behind
    Are making Boobela gasp –

I switch to scary-calming voice –
    'Keep looking straight ahead,
It won't go on forever, trust me' –
    And *pray* her nerve will hold.

The sky erupts in white and blue!
    And Boobela breathes and stops;
Mum takes the wheel and Boobela slumps
    While I'm still reading maps.

It all goes swimmingly … until
    The road begins to rise
And Mum blurts out, 'My vertigo!'
    And stops, and gently cries.

Boobela, shredded, can't believe it
    Nor can Mum and me.
We bale out in a horrid silence
    And gaze at plains below.

Then Boobela opens up the boot
    Sighing like a scirocco
And rummages around her bag
    To find her Jameson's bottle.

She screws the top off, takes a slug
    And lets the liquid burn …
She licks her lips, another glug
    Like a baddie in *High Noon*.

She thrusts it at me: 'Does you good!'
    And takes the driver's wheel.
My first and second whiskeys sear me
    As we roar up the hill.

So we progress with other selves:
    Mum quiet, feeling guilty;
Boobela calm except when she
    Starts laughing hysterically.

And I have left behind the sphere
    Of essays, prose and poetry –
Now nothing matters but the map
    That's vainly trying to read me.

ACT II

The Burnd Lampe
Portugal Street
September 1977–June 1978

Since God confines all things within due order,
what place can be left for random processes?
—Boethius, *Consolation of Philosophy*, Bk. 5.1

Brother

Michaelmas term, 4 October 1977

We've started off as brothers,
John driving, elbow on the window,
A glowing roll-up in his fingers
And belting out 'John Barleycorn';
Me thinking of the coming term,
A not-quite-fresh man, a one-year vet,
Anxious to slow the cycle down:
Let me be scholarly, but not yet …
Royston, Foxton, Harston –
The Anglo-Saxon *tuns* are waymarks
To fields that widen vastly, flatten
Into a wilderness of otherness –
Church towers on the skyline,
Crowns of trees with aureoles of rooks.
My stomach's churning.
    The spires of Cambridge break
The silence. In my new accommodation,
A residential terraced area –
I'm now an exile from the Fountain,
Three roads away. Siberia.
But still we are two brothers …
Until the moment of goodbye –
I'm at the window waving like a mother
Then taking out my student guise
I unpack books, begin to shelve them
But thinking all the time of John
Accelerating to his realm –
A pub, a music gig in London,
And how I'd love to be among
That seedy Southall glitz –
To hear him breaking into song
As 'Stan Francisco and the Golden Gits'.

Tenant

In Portugal Street

In lieu of mum she counts as mum,
Mrs Parker, a benign cockatrice
Of bedder-matron-aunt,
A childless widow squeezing grief
Or loss into her pancaked cheeks.
I watch her from my window –
Her hair a bulb of conker-sheen –
As she trundles her shopping trolley
With fingers made of knuckles –
I wait until the front door slams
With an aftermath of tuttings –
A starting gun for me to resume
My essay on the madness of John Clare.
She spoils me, and I can sense her
Lingering after I've closed my door –
Always keen for hallway chatter …
Except the time I didn't shut her fridge
And made her steak smell high –
She tried so hard to bite her tongue
But bit my head off, tears in eyes …
That still pursue me from when
I left her in the summer. She said:
'You'll come and visit me again?'
'Of course I will.' I swear I meant it.
'That's what they always say,' she said.
'I *will*.' I kept repeating it.
'Of course I will.' So easy to say –
I still rehearse it, can't erase
Her smile so eager to believe me
Her crow's feet tightening her eyes.

Tryst

At Trinity Bridge, 9 October 1977

The clocks are striking eight around the town.
I stare along the bridge to New Court arch,
Willing her silhouette to get here soon …

I mutter my lines – like Jacques' lover
'Sighing like furnace, with a woeful ballad
Made to his mistress' eyebrows'. A shiver

Creeps in my scarf and down my jumper
Each minute till eight-thirty, forty-five, and nine.
But I have visualised our brief encounter

So intensely – that when I cross the bridge
To go back to my digs, resigned,
I pass our doppelgängers as they watch

The river, and quiver at my fleeting ghost
To whom they owe their moment of existence.

Love in a Cambridge Climate

1. Fewer

After Pierre de Ronsard's chanson 'Le printemps n'a point tant des fleurs'

The Mathematical Bridge has fewer angles
And Parker's Pieces fewer blades of grass
And Fitzbillies fewer Chelsea buns
The Seeley Library fewer panes of glass
There are fewer bricks in the U.L.
And fewer blue stockings in Girton
And fewer finials on King's Chapel
And fewer pints drawn in the Baron
Trinity has fewer Nobel prizes
And Kettle's Yard fewer surprises
Than pangs in my heart for you,
My Love, pangs in my heart for you.

2. On the Sidgwick Site

After Pierre de Ronsard, 'L'autre jour que j'estois sur le haut d'un degré'

I heard your moped first, in Sidgwick Avenue,
As I was walking from a morning lecture
On Dylan by Professor Ricks, then saw you –
You glanced my way as you took off your helmet
And sent a beam of light, an airy splinter
That pierced my soul, printing you in my heart –
A flash, it was, a lightning jag that fractures
Clouds, turning Cambridge from dark to dazzle –
Enough to shiver me, as if I had a fever.
My saving grace lay in your moon-white hand –
I saw it wave (though I was blinded, frazzled),
A flicker – a sign I hoped of your affection
That saved me from the dance of pain and joy
You had inflicted with your solar eye.

Playwright

1. Chemistry

Rehearsing my play, *The New Oracle*

The Spade and Beckett bar,
A quiet corner, Phil and me.
His ginger mop and walrus moustache
Take gravity too seriously.
He gets jokes, doesn't do laughing,
Frets about his raison d'être –
'Why did I come to *Magdalene*?'
'Why am I doing English Lit?'
Incapable of bluster or front
He's staring at my script.
Another swig of Double Diamond –
I'm squiffy, sounding off: 'Fate!
Got to trust it guides you to …
Right time, person, place,
Alignment of the planets.
It's like tuning in … you need faith.
Got to trust, open up yourself
Or else you'll live in randomness,
A life of tumbling accidents.
Computer dating's ludicrous!
What can you tell from someone's tastes?
You'll likely be compatible
Over choice of toothpaste
As culture … Jesus or … Purcell.'
   A Hamlet of sighs, hesitations,
Phil can't be bothered to indulge me.
I ask about his own romances –
He blurts he hasn't had one. 'Surely
You've chatted someone up?'

He exhales, covers me in smoke,
Glares; reverts to glum.
I do a laugh and buy more pints
Then listen as he reads the male lead
On a computer date – with such *duende*
I sober up. He's doing what I dread.
For I can see that he's not acting –
He may not even know what 'acting' is –
He's daring to expose his soul
And jumping into the abyss
Of every moment that he's never known.

2. The Prompter

On directing my play, *The New Oracle* at Trinity theatre,
3 December 1977

I'm in the wings with Anne, relaxed
After her pre-performance vomit.
Phil's on stage – first computer date –
Tweaks his beard, checks his watch.
Three nights of playing God!
Thank me I'm nearly done.
Just one more hour for Phil and Anne
To live the lives I've given them.
And I am ready with the script
To check each word, fill each pause;
I know what happens in the end.
What might have been remains
In screwed-up bits of paper in a bin.

House lights: rapid smacks of clapping,
'She loves you, yeah, yeah, yeah,'
Ushers the audience into Great Court
While we go drinking in the Mitre –
And after pints I get the creepy sense
For all our careless quick-fire repartee
There's Someone watching us
Off stage, always just a line ahead,
Laughing at our lit-up flirty banter
And hopes, and all in light of knowing
The corkscrew of our lives
Already written to the bitter end.

Scholar

1. Tutorial

I don't know who is less at ease –
Me ... or Mr Leo Salingar
Squaring the world through black-framed glasses
Behind a desk full of clutter,
Miasma of stale tobacco
Kippering his stacks of books.
A trial neither can prepare for –
A seventeenth-century text:
He waits for me to offer thoughts
I've failed to form; I wait for him
To offer thoughts between coughs
And see him in a Restoration wig
Perusing Samuel Pepys's *Diary*,
Decanter on desk, cat beside fire.
It's wrong he has to stare at me,
Be-denimed youth with greasy hair
Desperate not to look him in the face.

No shifting the Restoration text
Resigned he takes a silver case
And offers me a fag, a Navy Cut –
We light them from the same Swan Vesta,
Sit back and let our lazy exhalations
Entwine in mutual space and cover
Our differences, reducing us
To what we are: a silence of two blokes,
Taking a moment, having a smoke.

2. Diviner

On first reading T.S. Eliot's *Collected Poems*

The frowning-crease above my nose
Is like the author's on the cover.
Could this be the one? I flick through pages
And place my finger in at random:
Where is the Life we have lost in living?
Where is the knowledge we have lost in information?
The cycles of Heaven in twenty centuries
Bring us farther from God and nearer to the Dust -
A stirring, deep down, or in the dark –
Like our tortoise in the spring, in attic straw,
Or a wren flickering on a hawthorn branch.
Is this what I've been waiting for?
I dare to pick another random page –
It's like the Sortes Virgilianae. Here goes:
And the wind shall say: 'Here were decent godless people:
Their only monument the asphalt road
And a thousand lost golf balls.'
This is my Weltanschauung! I close
The book ... then open it, and read once more:
I said to my soul, be still, and wait without hope
For hope would be hope for the wrong thing ...
How can it agitate me like this
And dissipate the interference
Between myself and anamnesis?
Like moving up your finger vertically
And lightly on guitar strings
Caressing frets to discord till
The magic twelfth one rings –
Your pick trills off harmonics –
A shivering that sings your heart
And your soul clicks
With what it knows not what.

3. On First Finding Jung's *Collected Works* in Trinity Library

Much had I travelled in reams of words
Of Chaucer, Keats and Tennyson
Before that day when I discovered
In the gloaming of the library storeroom –
Packed tight along a shelf like bullion –
That cache of weighty hardback tomes –
I opened one – such words flashed out! –
*Mandala, alchemy, the shadow,
Synchronicity* and *anima* …
                       Then I felt
Like Howard Carter gazing through
A peephole in the tomb of Tutankhamun –
And asked if there was something he could see
(As silence clutched the Valley of the Kings)
Could only mutter:
                    'Yes. *Wonderful things.*'

4. Slave

In Gonville and Caius

I nearly see my features
In the high black boots
That guard his door
Like glossy faithful hounds.
A raspy whisper
Responding to my knock
Invites me to enter;
His feet in blue silk socks
Adorn a footstool cushion;
A pale hand gestures
To a chair before his throne.
I take a scruff of papers,
Begin to read aloud
My thoughts on Nietzsche;
I keep pausing for a nod,
A biscuit tossed my way.
He presses fingertips
Into a thoughtful cage
As if to trap my hopes …
After what seems an age,
My stomach in a clench,
He ranges happily
On *Übermensch*
And slave morality.
I'm so relieved. I sit
And grin like an idiot
And cannot wait to spit
And shine his boots.

5. The Weekly Essay

Is like hearing a 'Last call for passengers …'
While scribbling on an emigration form
Or skimming instructions on a fire extinguisher
While smoke is oozing under the door
Or late-night leafing through *Britannica*
Forgetting what it is you're looking for …
The weekly essay makes me crave the time

    To idle   in Burnt Norton

    The rose garden   the empty pool

    Filling with light   and time

    To stroll with Yeats   through San Vitale

    Absorbing gold from tesserae   and time

    To hear the silence   in the railway carriage

    At Adlestrop   and from afar

    The songs of birds   of Oxfordshire

    And Gloucestershire.

Sic Transit

I turn my back, return to college –
And Mum informs me that we've moved to *Wiltshire*.
A house beside a stream with watercress,
A nearby cricket pitch, the Fox and Goose;
George Herbert's vicarage six miles away.
But no more Dad.
                        He'd visit us on Sundays –
A tantalising breeze-in after tennis.
I'll miss his chutzpah, beaming face –
A rhythm or a still point in the drift
Of all this traffic of acquaintances
And shift of student rooms and moving house.

His presence was a memory of slow death.
His absence is a fading afterlife:
A slamming car door, song … footsteps on the drive.

Ghosts

21st birthday dinner, Garrick Club, 9 December 1977

'To destroy the illusion is really to spoil the whole play.'
—Erasmus, *Praise of Folly*

We're in Dad's theatre: a member's room,
An oval table, silver on the cloth;
I'm girded by such kindly phantoms.
Beside me is my ex – who's still a ghost –
But half-remembering what was lost
She reaches for my hand below the table
And finger-taps a morse of embered love.
And Olly soon to leave my life, has left
Already in his heart. His eyes are glazed –
So ill at ease with all this extraversion,
His body functioning, his spirit at a loss
Planets away. And dear old Jonesy, lonely
At Oxford and his house at Wolvercote,
Unsettled by a lack of purpose, a lack
Of friends, the selling of his childhood home.
But now, for me, he's putting on an act.
And Caroline, an old friend up at Girton,
Blinking at this bubbly festiveness,
Blanking the violence done to her in India,
Politely listening, politely listless
While roaming numbly through the Punjab.
And then my family – full complement –
With Mum and Dad together again,
Remembering the roles of happy parents –
I have to jog myself it isn't real:
I'm watching a materialised memory
Or vision of what might have been.
And I bless each player for this make-believe.

Orpheus

Ted Hughes at the Hobson Gallery to celebrate
the Leonard Baskin exhibition, 27 February 1978

Baskin's birds are screaming from their frames.
Two lads in front of me and Olly
Whip up their self-euphoria: 'He'll burst in
Flapping his arms, dressed as Crow' –
'Yeah, black shawl on his head, fake beak.'
The MC tells us like a funeral notice:
'Ted's snowed up in Devon; he'll come next week.'

And so we congregate again like addicts
Or members of an esoteric cult,
Baskin's birds still screaming from their frames.
Ted's late. Perhaps he'll never turn up.
We tread time, loosen grizzly yawns –
Until three women clad in furs burst in
Hauling a slab of Yorkshire granite –
A mop of floppy hair, big sideburns,
Down-turned eyes. It takes a seat;
And doesn't have to read a word of *Crow*
Because it's just *Big Ted* ... growling
And drawling until we're flying to Siberia –
His Calder Valley-transatlantic vowels

Create a cave   a fire   a drumming shaman

Who turns us into elders, rapt, blinking,

While from their frames

Baskin's birds are listening.

Refugee

At Wolfson Court, Girton College hostel

The light of a conservatory
    Even in winter, and the cosiness
    And soapy warmth of a launderette;
Soft corridors of girls off duty
In T-shirts, slippers, dungarees,
    Boiling kettles, peering into fridges.
    A rainbow in Calvin Cambridge
A crock of gold for boarding refugees
Like me, attracted to the sisterhood
    Of Marian, her hair a-froth with curls
    A Sydney-Harbour-Bridge of a smile
Dispensing gin on tap and Marlboros
Like the jazziest doctor in the cosmos;
    And long-haired Anne so febrile-foxy
    And Gill part girl part bush-baby
And Ca the Scottish convent lass,
Mortician pale, shrieking in fun or agony –
    So finely balanced you never know;
    My Kiwi girlfriend Sarah O
Laid back and always late but lovely
In her flowing bougainvillea dress
    And long hair fanning across the dance floor.
    In Marian's room, exams are just a rumour:
We slouch on carpet, bed or chairs
Amid the shush of tonic water, Joni's
    'Oh, I wish I had a river I could skate away on',
    Blue curls of smoke, the winter sun
Diminishing the day in cold degrees …

Spectator

1. Letting Go

On seeing my play, *The New Oracle*, performed at Oxford,
11 March 1978

A shock to see her acting someone else –
My love of only months ago – I feel
As if I'm spying from the audience;
The hazel eyes I gazed in for so long
Are now a gift for strangers – the smile
That captured me when meeting her in Ealing,
A blaring party, three girls facing me –
I yelled if one of them would like to dance
And felt like Paris wanting Aphrodite.
She took my hand before she really knew
What she was doing and made a mess
Of both our callow hearts, who recognised
The other as the future closing in

As now they feel the past, widening.

2. Tragi-Comedy

Antigone, Girton Drama Society, Easter Term, 14 March 1978

Lights go out:
Antigone stands
In dark
Her world collapsed
But poised to break
Our hearts –
The spotlight
Primed
To make her face
A moon-mask.
Nemesis!
Something slips:
The spotlight hits
Her *kneecaps*
Then quivers up
And up to light
Her face, quivery
Trying to fight
The laughter-shriek –
The audience
Bite knuckles …
And Zeus alone
Knows how
Antigone
Keeps going
When everyone
Has gone
In agony.

Summer Term

14 April, 1978

Begins mid spring: days of moon-white suns
The punts still smoky in their pens
And trees along the Backs pubescent green.

At first, insouciance of students, phoney war;
But sombreness will gather day by day –
As if there's talk conscription's on the way.

Eleusinian

Tea with I.A. Richards, Magdalene Fellows' Garden, 20 May 1978

He's watching the 1920s in a slideshow
Across the river's screen, recalling years
As if they're happening around us now.

His wife pours out the tea. We sip, at leisure
Among the flowers and shrubs; the willow's hair
Cascades and flicks the surface of the water.

'Is there anything in life that you regret?'
Long pause. Perhaps I've been too intimate?

'Neglecting Classics for English. What's your subject?'
'English. I changed from Classics.' He laughs.

We fall silent, like old initiates
Remembering the mysteries of Eleusis

And how it felt to live in Otherness
And how it feels to live in loss.

The Statues

In the Museum of Classical Archaeology, 27 May, 1977

For Adrian Poole

Are standing there as if they're waiting for me,
As if I'd told them I'd popped out for bread
And took a year to make my homeward journey.

I don't know how to look at these old friends
Emerging from my psyche: as I turn
Each freezes in a game of Grandma's Footsteps.

They never left me: my archaic smile –
A sort of glazed unthinking curl of lips –
Is lighting up the face of Kleobis, while

Like me he's taking an initial step, alert,
Unsure about this new reality
And wondering if the ground will bear his weight.

There's poor old Herakles, marooned in muscle,
Exhausted, leaning on his bludgeon-club
And musing, as I am, how life can dwindle –

For him a grind of smash-and-grab, for me
A weekly shrinking from Nemean lions
Into books. And there's my friend from Delphi!

The Bronze Charioteer, still cool and calm:
'Restraint under pressure!' Spunky Dunky shouted
Flashing up the slide of him in class

And dutifully we aped this glacial hero,
Made sure our schooled pain, pressure, panic,
Weren't worthy of a blinking of an eye.

And, look, Myrrhine on a funeral vase,
So delicate and pretty; she looks nineteen,
Her eyes cast down, the sort of lass

I'd take to parties – now she's led by Hermes
Who takes her gently by the hand
As if to say *death is easy, trust me.*

Her relatives are saying their goodbyes
As Hermes now prepares to fly her off
To somewhere where each moment's a surprise –

Where feelings, thoughts, have been removed
From everything familiar, her life –
And mine – must start anew, must start anew.

Poet

1. Revised Myth

Entry for the Powell Prize, 1 June 1978

The snake lay still, the essence
Of snake generations compressed
Into each atom of nerve and muscle;
Its oily green coils glistening
With the dryness of glazed paint.
The warm-blooded serene saint
Leant over and let drip drops of holy water
Until like a fork of lightning spasm
The snake, crucified, spat and spat
Back the gospel with hiss and venom,
Its blind tongue flickering foil-like,
Head and tail split from each other
By the great sackweight of solid flesh.
Unpeeling itself, it began to shudder,
Then rocketed through the bracken
That crackled like rain on a live rail.

Wherever he went, the snakes vanished:
He lobbed a cross.
They darted into foxholes.
He clicked his fingers,
They slipped between the cracks of gravestones.
He mouthed 'Abracadabra',
They melted into their own mirages.

But while the saint kicked off his sandals
The snakes chewed their way through thick earth,
And they met, and snake ate snake
Until just one serpent, sweating in its juices,

Its back crusted with the hills of Ireland,
Lay still.
And now it lies waiting,
Swelling under the thin skin of the New Testament,
Waiting for the saints on St Peter's
To drop off, one by one,
Like stand-up ducks at a rifle range.

2. Snakes

I don't know how the snakes arrived
    Or why they were so tenacious.
I scribbled – just to see what happened next
    And watched in fascination as the phrases
Slithered off to find their paths.
    My first-ever poem it seemed to me
Would be my last –
    A rush of blood, a boyish *jeu d'esprit*.
Yet there was something in the process …
    The unpredicted mini raptures –
A shifting to another universe
    In which laws and language seemed to alter
Each time I blinked, remembering
    To wait and let the words re-cast themselves
Until they stepped into the fullness of their being.
    And surely all of life can be like this –
An emptying of self, a stepping into the strangeness
    Of never knowing what comes next.

The Burnd Lampe

English Tripos Part I, Paper 2, 26 May 1978

Questions flash by as if I'm drowning –
'In what sense may Restoration drama
Be called a coterie art?' 'Discuss' 'Compare'
'Do not use the same material twice'
'Offer an account of the relationship between
Serious didactic purpose and spectacle ...'
'Do not use the same material twice' –
I can't think of any material *once*
And time is ticking like a death-watch beetle
I push and push the questions down
As if I'm trying to surface from a lake –
And then a blur – a piece called *Nosce te ipsum* –
'And yet, alas, when all our Lampes are burnd,
Our bodies wasted, and our spirits spent ...
It's like the author's whispering to me
To help me get my head above the water
When we have all the learnéd Volumes turnd,
Which yeeld mens wits both helpe, and ornament;
What can we know? or what can we discerne?
I'm nearly at the surface – still a blur –
I need oxygen oxygen and clarity
When Error chokes the windowes of the mind:
The diverse forms of things how can we learne,
That have bene ever from our birth day blind?'

Party Animal

Wolfson Court, 6 June 1978

Nobody knows Anne's poured a bottle
Of Tennessee 100% proof liquor
Into the punchbowl to ignite the party;
And Olly, me and Marian's father,
A tough-nut Aussie, big in business,
And Rob, who's Marian's fella,
Are stilting smalltalk, getting poison-pissed
And sweating from the chilli con carne.
The evil Circe brew's reducing us
To spines with limp Tyrannosaurus arms
And words that need speech therapy;
Poor Marian's dad – I feel for him!
He's come from London just to see
His daughter and her friends and sip Lapsang.
Now look at him – with Sarah O and Ca
Around his shoulders singing songs
Directly in his fuzzy-haired ears
Compelling him to join the chorus
Of 'Waltzing Matilda – Waltzing Matilda' –
I'd laugh or cry but am bemused by Gill
Who's standing face against the wall –
She whips around as if in a huff
And leaves a streaky arc of colour –
A comet of carne – then staggers off –
I stumble out myself to find a toilet
And spot an open door – inside
Gill's flat out, corpse-like, on her bed
I sit beside her, checking she's alive –
I'm peering in her eyes when Sarah passes
And sees me she imagines kissing Gill,
Storms in and slaps my cheek so hard
It looks as if an iron's pressed it.

I make it back and Marian's dad
Tries sneaking out but is recaptured
And forced to bop to Chaka Khan –
I look at Olly and one of us is shouting –
'We gotta get out of this place' –
We're far too gone, it's sink or sink.
As if we're last in some three-legged race
We bumble off, arms interlinked,
But cannot find the mirage of the exit;
We titter round the swaying corridors
Like two lost tipsy polar bears;
And girls in rooms with open doors
Observe us coolly as we limp on past
And one with raven hair and glasses,
Who studies Norse, whom Olly fancies,
Comes out to witness our slow-motion race –
A tragic Tour de Wolfson Court –
And Olly proposes marriage to her –
I drag him off while he is shouting
'I'm serious, I'm really *really* serious …'
Eventually we find the exit door
And see
         the summer stars, the Milky Way –
We guide ourselves by chapel spire
To Garret Hostel Lane and Trinity
Arm in arm, singing in between the splutters
Of every gurgly laugh
And feeling we could walk forever

Like Oates and Wilson in the afterlife.

Fairy Godmother

On being a steward at the Trinity May Ball, 15 June 1978

An hour before it starts I'm given a box
Of passes. A box of gold dust. Incredible.
I'd like to scatter them in Market Square
And watch them do what breadcrumbs do to pigeons.
Instead I scurry off, jump on my saddle
Like Robin Hood dropping on his horse
From an overhanging branch and skedaddle –
My tailcoat flapping like two ailerons –
To Thompson's Lane and Olly's eyrie.
I scale the staircase, hammer on his door –
His bird's nest and speccy eyes appear –
'Whatcha doing tonight?' I giggle-slur –
His eyebrows twitch – 'I'll bloody tell you what –
You're *only* going to … the Trinity Ball.'

Then flying off like Hermes I cross the Cam
And get to Wolfson Court, red-faced and panting;
I burst into the common room:
Sarah's watching *Top of the Pops* with Marian –
They gawp as if I'm a celebrity
Who's broken out of the TV screen.
'The ball … You're going to it … *Trinity*.'

My steward duties mean an hour on,
An hour off – enough to roam and hear
Elvis Costello and the Attractions croon
'*I don't WANna GO to CHELsea*' …
While in the disco tent a voice is shrieking
'*Whether you're a brother or whether you're a mother
You're stayin' alive, stayin' alive!*'

Feel the city breakin' and everybody shakin',
You're staying alive, staying alive!"
And look! there's Olly doing clownish dances
Bent-legged like Groucho Marx; and Marian
And Sarah floating happy and glorious
As if they've been transformed to photons …

As if pure joy can never come to pass
Unless an ambush makes you you-less –
And suddenly you're music, dancer, dance,
And all the laws of nature cease –

Newton's apple hanging in the air

The setting sun become the rising sun

A gold balloon arcing from the river

Through a mist of atomised champagne.

SECOND INTERMISSION

Rough Beast

My first time on an aeroplane
    And Jonesy quick as a flash
Grips me and splutters as we taxi
    'Handbrake's off – we'll crash!'

Then high up as we scarily bank
    He spots another weakness:
'Your big fat weight! – lean inwards *now*!' –
    I throw myself across.

He's still chuckling in Corfu
    And our cottage on the hill –
We have no electricity,
    And get water from a well.

But university recedes
    Before the dry cicadas
And Greeks who greet us with a smile
    And sunny '*Kaliméra*s'.

Each day we go to Paleocastrítsa
    To swim and loll at ease
While Tom our painter friend and host
    Is sketching olive trees.

And drinks alone so secretly
    We're caught out on the hop –
One evening when we're eating supper
    His forehead hits his soup.

Next night we take him to a disco –
　　To do him a bit of good –
But after dancing like a Bacchant
　　He bolts off up the road.

We bolt off too, but he's too fast –
　　We hear him up ahead –
His footsteps pounding out the yards
　　In a tom-tom of dread.

I fear we'll find the house in flames
　　Or maybe something worse;
But when we get there, breathing hard,
　　We hear the strangest voice –

Reciting ritually 'The falcon
　　Cannot hear the falconer …
Things fall apart …' and there he is –
　　Commanding the verandah.

We stand and watch and let him roar
　　To diabolic shadows;
Eventually he goes inside
　　And we sneak in like ghosts.

Next day at breakfast he's all smiles,
　　The night before erased;
He cuts a peach and offers it
　　And doesn't seem half crazed.

He then goes off to paint his world
　　Of sunlit groves and skies;
But always through his canvas come
　　Two rising demon eyes.

ACT III

Days of Lazy Punting

Great Court
September 1978–June 1979

All of us must make our exit nonetheless ...
Others will always take our place.
And this is how we mortals survive as a species –
It's like a river staying in its bed although its waters
    keep on flowing.
— John of Salisbury, *Policraticus*, Bk. III

Questioner

2 October 1978, Michaelmas Term

The Fens are amplifying the sky
Above the long straight Baldock Road.
I'm in Dad's car without his company,
Just his company driver, Charles,
Black-suited stocky Londoner,
An overhanging brow, a boxer's nose.
He's chatty: 'Makes you wonder –
If God exists – one year, three popes!'
I'm thinking it's one year, three terms,
Before I leave the Cambridge masque
Already rueing stuff I haven't done
And things done badly. I'll depart
Just as I get to know my character.
'I mean if God can't save his own …
What d'you think – you're clever?'
What *do* I think? I don't know.
I've slid into not 'thinking' thinking
For two years, apart from Jung
And dimly sense my soul groaning
Beneath the decencies of literature,
Homeric pub crawls, parties;
As for God – I just don't know;
I'd *love* to know.
                    We enter the city,
My last year crowding into view.
At Trinity I wave Charles off
Amused to think it might be thought
My dad's a gangster or a bailiff.
My final room's in Great Court! –
I'm like a Tudor king, or lord of the manor …

Until I find my angular garret
Squatting atop a winding stair.
The window's open, the bed's soft ...
Charles, God, three popes –
Is God the Clockmaker, winding up the cosmos
Then watching through a telescope?
Is God an entity, a spirit or a process?

A blade of sun cuts the windowsill;
Outside, the fountain's harpsichord
Is dripping rounds of sparkling notes,
A tingling steady-state sonata
In which there's no beginning or end
From alpha to omega, alpha to omega,
Alpha to Omega ...

And maybe that's my answer.

Rocker

Budgie concert, Corn Exchange, 30 October 1978

My Teens have finally tracked me down!
A crowd of geezers, fingers stuck in jeans,
Their pony tails and tresses dipped in chip-pans –
Five years they've been pursuing me
Five years since smoking with my mates
To 'Bring me round with whiskey glitter' – the band
Now resurrect their riffing hit
'We're All in the Grip of a Tyre-fitter's Hand' –
I pluck and strum my trusty Stratocaster
A memory of an amputated bone
Then stop. It's all too much, grotesque!
How can I feel so old at twenty-one?
So comfy with these motorbiking gits? –
What's wrong with Punk – why can't I like
The Pistols, X-Ray Spex, the Slits?
I scan the hall. No one I recognise.
I start to chant, 'She's Hot as a Docker's Armpit';
And as I sing I see the Seven Hills Road,
The lay-by where we used to hitch to Guildford –
The golden road to Samarkand –
The Civic Hall, and Budgie in their glory,
Spotlights shedding gold, a swaying crowd,
The aftermath of zingy ringing ears,
A friend's friend revving the Cortina –
No seat belts and the driver drunk –
Towards the future
The Cambridge Corn Exchange, a head shaking,
A straining voice
A soul begging for the coup de grace.

Revenant

Moonlight in Great Court; after hours of
Valhalla swilling in the Baron of Beef
To drown a break-up, fractious fickle love,
I see a light on in my room. A thief?
Someone purloining my research on Yeats?
Or lying in wait to drink sherry, beer,
Then spout like a gargoyle through the night?

I burst in ... there she is, just sitting there.

Her pale long neck, magenta dress,
Aglow in lamplight; her face in shadow.
Surely those bitter words have done for us?
The silence grows.
She looks up: 'I only came to say
This last year wouldn't be the same without you.'

The University Library

Lent Term, 1979

For Thomas McCarthy

Its tower rises in the winter rain,
Brick sculpture of Cape Canaveral,
A power station that burns on brains.
Inside, a labyrinth without a centre –
I ought to lay a trail of crumbs
To get back to the lobby area
But shuffle through the aisles and rooms
Alert for any scholar in a corner
With slicked-back hair, war-time suit,
Staring at me as if I'm transparent.
The thought of being here at night! –
Alone with millions of authors
Mouldering in un-remembrance –
Believing they can only come to life
From all the stacks of catacombs
If they're exposed to mortal eyes ...

Now it's closing time. The corridors
Are emptying; silence deepens –
Apart from what my inner ear can hear:
A shuffling sound or creeping –
As when outside the mouth of Hades
Odysseus poured blood in a trench
Then listened for the coming of the shades
To drink their substance back again.

Death of a Thespian

1. 'The Infernal Machine'

Lent Term, 24 February 1979

Striding out in All Saints Passage
I spot laconic cool Camilla
And hope to chat for long enough
To gaze into her sapphire eyes
And guess their twitches of irony.
She waltzes past me, turns and barks
'Woof! Woof!', walks on –
Her shoulders rippling with laughter –
She must have seen me act last night.
I thought I was so suave! –
Anubis in black tie, Sobrané cigarette,
A dashing jackal mask.

I watch her gliding on – her hair
As shimmery as Cleopatra's –
And want to shout my lines at her:
'Our time is folded in eternity!
And as the God of the Dead, I
Can see your life unfold –
Stretch out in front of me,
A picture in a single dimension.
All episodes from birth to death
Are pinpricks in Time's cloth!'
Instead I stand there yelp-less –
'Woof! Woof!' the epitaph
Of my career in acting. I watch her
Diminishing on the path – and I
No longer jackal god but mortal cur,
Tail between my legs, nose dry.

2. Cast Party

After my play Who Killed Cassandra?, *6 March 1979*

For Harry and Stephen

Satyr play with drink instead of speech;
The set a high-camp room in Magdalene,
The priestly candles on the mantelpiece
Flare to the Liebestod from *Tristan*;
A squash of us dissolving egos
In cheap red wine – an etching acid,
A mordant biting through personae
Reducing us to pure instinctual id
Unpeeling our vacuity:
Uptight Bruce gyrates, shirtless, stung
By Wesley whipping him with a tie
As gently as a tabby's flicking tongue;
Confessors bawl at priests who shout
Their absolution; a couple go to ground
And kiss forever since they lack
The will to break the seal of their mouths.

This is the play – not the one an hour ago –
Our words now slurred or spat
In breathalyser speech, but still an impro –
The freedom of a world without a script –
No plot, no lines can be rehearsed –
And we can bruit prophetic truths
Nostrils flared, at ease with Cassandra's curse
That no one will believe our crazy words.

Regretter

Last summer term, 18 April 1979

My train is slowing down, the sign
Unblurs to 'Cambridge'. Laden like a yak
I ask a motorist for a lift to town –
'You're young: should damn well walk.'
A wintry start to summer term in spring.
The omens are reversing. I walk along
The top of Trumpington, regretting
What might have been, and stuff not done
Like cricket at Fenner's, Kettle's Yard,
A pint of double helix in the Eagle,
A mille-feuille from Fitzbillies. I pass
Peterhouse, St Catz, the Copper Kettle –
Still unfamiliar – I've hardly strayed
A hundred yards from Trinity Street.
Outside the window of Belinda's
I watch new epicureans drink tea
And worship God the Cheesecake.
At Heffers I don't recognise the names
Of books displayed; freshers at the gate
Are far too cosy after just two terms.
I feel like … denim fluff from my navel
Who came, saw, conquered nothing.
It's weird that summer always has the feel
Of leaving somewhere, always leaving …
The lime-green chestnuts in full sail
Will sweep us off to futures unimaginable;
Except they won't be like these days
Of lazy punting I've never done at all.

Reviser

When exactly did it all begin –
This nodding at a friend instead of chatting?
And diving in a shop to miss someone
With whom I was quite intimate –
First year, they say, you're making mates
The last, you're trying to jettison them
Ridiculous the waste –
My soul's a land of discontent
And knows the great unravelling has started
And suddenly it all seems sad –
Gobbling quotes to stem my Finals dread
Shedding friends I never had.

Sundials
8 May 1979

Two years have passed; two summers with the length
Of two long winters – yet it seems like yesterday
Exploring Cambridge via random paths
And vistas, cul-de-sacs, allowing fate
To guide our progress, as we did in life.
Wherever you are, I'm on the trail again
A hungry ghost attempting to ritualise –
Or exorcise? – that sacred afternoon
Of heatwave. At St John's I step inside
Self-conscious déjà vus: unfripperied courts
Parterred with cobbles, jigsaw-puzzle neat,
The centre of the Bridge of Sighs – we paused
To watch the river glassing under us
And stared at punters turning, bumping boats
As if we were their guardian angels
Controlling their decisions with our thoughts.
Moving along the open stony corridors
I stop and bathe inside a grille of sunbeams;
A huge old almond doorway frames the lawns
We saw sweep down to moated Trinity.
    Back on the path to All Saints' Passage, Christ's –
We find the Fellows' garden, the sward a sheet
Tucked into shrubs, an Arden paradise –
I point out where I played in *As You Like It*,
The play you missed by only weeks,
Then lead you to the grove where Milton prayed
And heckled God for answers, grieving
For his belovéd soulmate Lycidas
Floating in the Irish Sea and decomposing –
O tides perform your restoration
And, O ye dolphins, waft the hapless youth ...

We wafted heat away, rejoined
The track and passed the 1640s sundial –
I Stand Amid ye Summer Flowers –
The gnomon was unable to reveal
How very soon *ye Passinge of ye Houres*
Would see our parting. On to Corpus Christi
And Old Court's medieval walls; I linger
Half-hoping for a sign or anomaly –
A monk, a limping fox, a snow-white deer
To amaze you with. The sun slips a cloud,
Spots the sundial on the wall beneath
The eaves, flames its golden crest and words:
Mundus transit et concupiscentia eius.

    In Silver Street the air – at last! – freshens,
Sun pulsing white behind the clouds,
The foamy weir rushing and thrashing,
I make my way towards the Granta pub
And settle on its awninged river terrace
To gaze at Lammas Land – fly-flicking cows,
Cracked mud, the sepia reeds and sedge
Along the treacly hem of scruffs of meadows –
The crumbliness that fades but never fades
In the amber of memory.

    We left, as I do now, and hugged the shade
Until the Fellows' Garden, Trinity;
We anchor under trees, and feel the coolness
Increasing … I grip your hand –
To stop you flying back to Balliol
Or Wolvercote, the Bodleian,
Or speeding through the lanes of Oxfordshire –
But it's too late. There's nothing more to do
Except lie back and let the leaves and branches
Move over me, the clouds move over me,
And dim the loss that time is always dimming.

Eventually I amble to the dial:
Ambulate in sapientia tempus redimentes –
But only love redeems, a light perpetual,
A sundial freed from shadow lines and numbers,
Pure disc of gold that's suddenly there
At nighttime rising as the harvest moon,
By day the blazing mirror of the sun.

Punter

To Grantchester

I drop the pole in vertically
And let it pierce the glaucous Cam
Until it touches silt – then twist it
And push and feel the surge upstream …
My first time in a punt; I'm anxious;
But Sarah O reclining in the back
Is playing cool – straw hat, long dress –
There's never been a person more relaxed!
We slip below the Bridge of Sighs
And past the honeycomb of Clare,
The sacred lawns of King's then glide
The other side of Silver Street weir …
Advancing till the city's a mirage
The atmospheric pressure of Finals
Lifting from banks of spriggy grass
And sprinkles of daisies, dandelions –
And so we penetrate the state

Of wordlessness and water shadows

And revel   in the space

The Zen
          of blank green
                              meadows.

Son

12 May 1979

Unlike Finals or some interview
I know each question, and every answer;
My father in a suit and Garrick tie,
My step-mum in a cocktail dress, fake fur,
Her golden hair swept back, a lioness
With blooded nails, a scent to scatter
Every creature in the forest.
We stroll by Neville's Court, the Backs;
I'm fighting surly silence; half dead
For weeks I want to see Dad right –
Fulfil his dream of me: the undergrad
In gracious rooms, toasting crumpets,
And making jokes about the Cambridge spies –
I know my raggy hair and denim jeans
Are not his Brideshead fantasy.
He's twitchy about his wife fitting in;
And she keeps winking randomly
As if I've dropped a smutty double entendre.
So it goes on. Small talk, bluster, clench
Of every muscle, neck downwards.
I serve tea but sense my attic's infra dig
With all its scary *books*. Eventually
It seems that Dad can't wait to exit,
And she can't wait to exit, and I ...
Feel unexpectedly deflated.
I see Dad roughly twice a year, at best –
Another chance to bond's evaporated.
I cannot guess
As I release him back into the wild
We'll have just twenty meetings left
Before I touch his hand at bedside
And listen to the snatchings of his breath.

Slough of Despond

Getting worse – this sleeping in until
    The afternoon not caring if I'm late
    For anything except the Pickerel
Or asylum in the folds of Wolfson Court.
    My cultural life has dwindled to
    The Damned (one evening at the Arts)
Emmanuelle (a Regal matinée).
    I'm not the type I think to get depressed.
    I shrug it off as hangovers, or possibly
Self-conscious Keatsian *tristesse*.
    My bedder comes in daily like a zookeeper
    To check for signs of breath
And tidy up my cage and turn my straw.
    I can't or won't dissect the problem –
    Finals-itis? Fear of leaving? Accidie?
Burn-out perhaps – the pressure of exams
    Since I was eight, the annual blight
    Forewarned by lengthening days of summer
And cricket shouts, trees of soft green light –
    I ought tell myself I'm free, nearly,
    Of years of seasonal cramming. Ought.
Meanwhile my conscience nags me,
    A voice I try ignoring or flooding out
    With bottles of Trinity sherry,
Insisting in dreams or semi-conscious states
    That only one thing's worthy of pursuit
    And it's not a First, 2:1, 2:2, but …
The holy spirit, God, Beauty, Truth,
    And only poetry will guide me to them.
    Now that I'm mired it all seems futile –
The essays, reading and exams –
    'Birth, and copulation, and death' –
    A three-year cycle over in a dream,

Like Bede's sparrow flitting from darkness
    Into a dining hall of feasting students,
    Enjoying a spot of light and warmth
Before returning to the dark again.

And how I wish I could've known back then
    This three-year manic poring over pages
    Would be of use, inform my future actions:
My mother driving me on pilgrimage
    To Eliot's East Coker and lost in a maze
    Of roads I quote the poem to find the village
And Mum explodes, 'This bloody lane
    Is *not* "insisting on the direction"!'
    Or sitting in Coole Park beside the lake
Imagining the ghosts of Yeats and Gonne
    And Lady Gregory's demolished home –
    Then startled by the rising white of swans
As if they are the page of Yeats's poem
    Leaving behind the print. Or driving to the Taw
    To find the spoor of Ted Hughes on a whim –
But on arrival feeling like a trespasser
    Skulking in the local shop, amazed
    And giggly to find a wine called 'Crow'.
Nor could I guess, foresee, how all these plays
    Would rescue me from public shyness,
    As when in Dublin's Concert Hall I'm frozen,
Queasy in the wings, poised to face
    Two thousand people glitteringly dressed –
    But then remembering I was Anubis
For heaven's sake! The God of the Dead –
    And all the lines I learned – while now
    In Dublin I'm myself: I only have to read.
I was too blinkered or benighted to know:
    Nothing is wasted. Not the boozy session
    In the Baron discussing Rennes-le-Château;

Nor jousting at the video game of 'Pong'
    Like Templars, in the Pickerel;
    Nor hiding in a wardrobe in St John's
For hours on end to crash the May Ball;
    Nor gazing at the Rubens in King's Chapel
    Amazed that cloth could look so gold and pliable.

Vain, vain! I study … beer mats, sherry labels
    And measure time in cups of Nescafé
    And Players No. 6 – or Camels
On feast days – and ransack Freud and Plato
    And Nietzsche for the 'English Moralists'.
    Finals galoom, libraries full of queues,
The U.L. like a rush-hour station, students
    Already acting like commuter-brokers;
    While on the Cam the punting tourists
Are playing students in their first week –
    Still dazed by otherworldly scenes, ignoring
    The little bumps and jolts and getting stuck,
Alive to every moment, and glorying.

The Eleventh Hour

1. The Losing Method

My desk has leaning towers of books
Filling me in, crowding me out,
Pulling me from pillar to post;
They're rearranging every thought
Insisting I must study more –
Each day I speed-read not enough
Yet what's enough I just don't know …
Then late at night I'm easing to
My underground curriculum –
Laozi is gently urging me to seek
My inner emptiness or chasm
And gaze at life in quietude:
All things, he says, are restless –
For doing is the essence of this world:
'Seek out non-action in yourself,
Descending to your inner root,
By finding stillness in the Way.
Students of books accumulate.
The Daoist *loses day by day*.'

2. The Night before Finals

My desk is flaked with papers; books disordered;
My armchair full of me, my ears listening
To Keats's poems on a tape recorder:

The blissful cloud of summer indolences
Benumb'd my eyes; my pulse grew less and less …
That's dangerous thinking! I sit on edge

And glow my ciggy down with dregs of coffee,
Fast-forward the tape to hypnotise
Myself with 'Sleep' and switch my thinking off:

O soothest Sleep! If so it pleases thee, close,
In midst of this thine hymn my willing eyes …'

I murmur this when pulling up my bedclothes –

Not life or death – *it's just an exam*! I'm calm.
I'm calm.
        Just like my clocks
                  and three alarms.

Endgame

1. Early Morning before Finals

I cannot stop
Reflecting on
The lad from Magdalene
Who cycled early
To the exam hall
To take his Finals
But when he reached
The railings
He simply pedalled
On and on
Along the London road
Until by midnight
He could hear
The sound of seagulls
Keening.

2. Final Time

Practical Criticism paper, 18 May 1979

I'm in a dream – some fella just like me
But not me turns the paper over –
'Compare this poem with at least two others'
And bloody hell his diary's been exposed –
'I have been laughing', it says, 'carousing,
Drinking late, sitting late, with my bosom cronies,
Oh, all are gone, the old familiar faces!'
He turns the page, another bit of poetry –
And Lordy it's another diary entry! –
'I sigh the lacke of many a thing I sought,
And with old woes new waile my deare times waste …
And weepe a fresh loves long since canceld woe …'
The me-not-me now scribble-scrawls off
Sentences in English that appear
In Arabic and knows that when he's stopped
The world will suddenly be different – he fears
The loss, that Trinity's about to sink
That he's about to hear 'Put down your pen'
And knows the dream is real and everything
Is coming to an

Our Revels

Magdalene May Ball, 13 June 1979

For a short while Fortune lets them use her costumes,
but when the pageant is over, they give back their bodies ...
—Lucian, *Menippus*

In Chesterton Lane within a shadow
I'm like a burglar dressed in white tie
My fingers interlaced to hoist up Sarah O
To scale the wall. Just too high!
I channel brother John, the crasher,
And walk to Magdalene Porters' Lodge:
A miracle – we look so right as revellers
That our immaculate disguise becomes
A mantle of invisibility
And somehow ... we simply stroll in
And smile at porters graciously –
Then burst out whooping, running
Into the Field of Cloth of Gold!
For everywhere the braided trees
Are lit with necklaces and diamonds;
On landing strips of lawns, marquees
Have dropped like snowy flyings saucers
In one of which we dance
To music by the Pasadena Orchestra –
'She's a Latin from Manhattan';
On the glitter of the river, punts sway
With the allure of Cleopatra's barge.
It's like ... VE Day –
The war with books and essays on the verge
Of ending in mad quaffs of wine
And Bacchic raving – God only knows
How many brain cells we're destroying
Imprinted with drama, prose and verse.

And yet it seems so necessary
To robe up for this final blast
And play the part of gala royalty
And slough our skins of three years
Of grotty student selves. We ease
Into states of tabulae rasae,
Drinking from fizzy streams of Lethe,
Ready for rebirth and becoming pupae
In some new scene.
                      By dawn we've flopped on grass
Like accident survivors, too dazed to care
About appearances: for now we are unmasked,
The cycle is complete –
                      the river
The cloud-capp'd towers, palaces, gardens,
And spires dissolving in the air –

An insubstantial pageant fading

The magic flitting from the theatre.

Last Rites

1.
Senate House noticeboard –
Exam results –
A writhe of seagulls scrapping
For crusts.

2.
I grasp the Praelector's proffered finger
That leads me to the wizard –
A Latin spell!
Releasing me releasing me ...

3.
A final stroll to the river,
Punts in their sheepfold, huddled
Against the wolf-howl
Of life.

The Magical Universe

24 June 1979

I exit Great Court – final time –
My dear old fountain tinkling goodbye
Like wind chimes, and cross the path of Simon,
An English grad I've rarely spoken to
Yet now we chat like best of friends.
I wonder what the future holds for him:
He's off to teach in Padua or Florence,
Offers to give his agency my name.
I laugh – me teaching *anybody*! –
And yet it's churlish not to play along.
I enter gateway-gloom, pass the Lodge
Like an actor after curtain calls
Retreating to the demi-light, applause
An echo in the creak of tip-up seats.
I keep my student costume, lose my mask.

What will stay from my performance?
Essays, tutors – Casey, Redpath, Ricks?
Latin grace, matriculation, graduation?
Or ... playing summer frisbee on the Backs
The afternoon when passers-by joined in?
Or Harry juggling crystal glasses,
Sangfroid when smashing them one by one;
Dressing up as newspapers for a party;
Cartoons for *Broadsheet* and *Stop Press*;
The first glimpse of my staircase name in gold;
Returning love-sick on the Oxford Bus
And thinking college seemed like home.
   My father gives his lights a double flash –
I brace myself for daddybadinage
As we depart from Life to life ... and

In the jerky silence of the car
I soon forget my words with Simon,
Can't guess what wizardry they'll wreak
Along the cosmic synapses –
Heracleion: the teachers Mike and Mick
Have been alerted to receive me;
The jeweller's daughter, Evyeneía,
Is revving up her turquoise limousine;
Maria might be seeing me already
In silty maps in tiny cups of coffee;
The schoolkids of Pyrgos, Rethymnon,
Are primed to start their chanting:
'We don't need no education.'
The tomb of Kazantzakis is waiting
To reveal its epitaph to me:
I do not hope for anything
I do not fear anything
I am free.

Two Rivers Press has been publishing in and about Reading since 1994. Founded by the artist Peter Hay (1951–2003), the press continues to delight readers, local and further afield, with its varied list of individually designed, thought-provoking books.